Sports Stars

RYNE SANDBERG

The Triple Threat

By Hal Lundgren

 CHILDRENS PRESS ®

CHICAGO

Cover photograph: Ira Golden
Inside photographs courtesy of the following:
Ira Golden, pages 6, 16, 18, 20, 29, and 40
Kevin W. Reece, pages 8, 10, 27, and 33
Bryan Yablonsky, pages 12, 25, 31, and 34
Vic Milton, pages 15, 38, and 42
G. Robarge, pages 22 and 36

Library of Congress Cataloging in Publication Data

Lundgren, Hal.
  Ryne Sandberg, the triple threat.

  (Sport stars)
  1. Sandberg, Ryne—Juvenile literature.
2. Baseball players—United States—Juvenile literature.
3. Chicago Cubs (Baseball team)—Juvenile literature.
I. Title. II. Series.
GV865.S2L86 1986   796.357'092'4 [B] [92] 85-29895
ISBN 0-516-04357-9

1 2 3 4 5 6 7 8 9 10 R 95 94 93 92 91 90 89 88 87 86

Sports Stars

RYNE SANDBERG

The Triple Threat

The 1984 baseball season started. Not many people had heard of Ryne Sandberg.

His family and friends knew of Ryne. They were in Spokane, Washington. He had been an All-City high school player. He was All-City in football and baseball. He went to Spokane's North Central High School. In football, he had been picked for the All-State team.

Ryne Sandberg's name was big in Reading, Pennsylvania. He was known in Oklahoma City, Oklahoma, too. He had played in the minors in those two cities.

Baseball fans in Chicago knew Ryne. He had played in the Cubs' infield in 1982 and 1983. He had done nicely. He batted and fielded well. He stole 69 bases those two years. But he was not a star. He wasn't even close to being a star.

Then the 1984 season started. Something was different in Chicago. Ryne Sandberg was a star.

He was at a new position. He was playing second base. He played it well. Just as well as he had played his old position, third base.

Pitchers still watched him when he was on base. He still might steal a base. But there was a big difference. The big difference was when Ryne came to bat.

Ryne was now a "tough out." When Ryne came to bat, the opposing pitcher knew he was in for a hard time.

What made Ryne different? Many things.

First, Ryne was improving. Kids improve every year. A 12-year-old plays Little League for one year. Then he gets better in his second year.

Major-league players aren't much different. When the 1984 season started, Ryne was 24 years old. That's young for a major leaguer. His improvement between 23 and 24 was awesome.

Jim Frey, the Cubs manager, wanted Ryne to swing harder at the ball.

Ryne changed the way he swung at the ball. The Cubs manager, Jim Frey, wanted Ryne to swing a little harder. Frey thought Ryne would hit more home runs. Hitting more home runs is good for a player. But sometimes a player then does not get as many singles. Manager Frey didn't feel this would happen to Ryne.

Mr. Frey was right. Wow, was he right! Ryne hit a total of 15 home runs in 1982 and 1983. By swinging harder in 1984, Ryne hit 19 home runs.

There was more good news. The hard swing didn't make Ryne strike out all the time. He didn't pop up all the time. He batted better than ever. In 1983 Ryne batted .261. In 1984 his average jumped to .314.

Fans remember the game against the St. Louis Cardinals. Ryne went to bat six times. He had five hits. The Cubs were losing, 9 to 8, in the ninth inning. Ryne hit a home run. The game was tied. The Cubs were losing again, 11 to 9, in the 10th inning. Ryne came to bat. A teammate was on base. Ryne hit his second home run. The game was tied again. The Cubs won the game in the 11th inning, 12 to 11.

Whitey Herzog is the Cardinal manager. After the game Herzog called Ryne "probably the greatest player I've ever seen."

The St. Louis Cardinal's manager called Ryne probably the greatest player he had ever seen.

Ryne is a good all-around player.

Ever played on a team? Then you can figure out how good Ryne really is. Did a kid on your team bat better than anyone else? Did a kid steal more bases than anyone else? Did a kid almost always make good catches and throws in the field? Was there a kid who usually made the big play just when you needed it?

Did your team have a player like this? Then your team was a little bit like the Chicago Cubs. Ryne Sandberg is *that* player for the Chicago Cubs. He can bat. He can field. And he can steal bases. He is a triple threat.

If the Cubs took a vote for their best hitter, best fielder, and best base runner, Ryne might win all three votes.

Now Ryne is more confident of his ability.

Ryne is a "natural."

The Cubs' "natural" helped them win the National League's Eastern Division. It was the Cubs first championship in 39 years. A manager cannot say one player is better than the other 24 players. That might hurt some other players' feelings. But Mr. Frey came close. He said, "No player has played as well for as long as Ryne has this season."

Baseball was played before the year 1900. But records of the game date back only to 1900. From 1900 until today is called baseball's "modern period."

Ryne G. hit singles, doubles, triples, *and* homers.

No player has had 200 or more hits plus 20 or more doubles, triples, home runs, and stolen bases in the same season. Not in baseball's modern period. But Ryne came close. He missed by only one triple and one home run in 1984.

Ryne smashed 200 hits. Thirty-six of the hits were doubles. Nineteen of the hits were triples and 19 were home runs. Men that hit with that power seldom run fast. But Ryne also stole 32 bases.

Only four other men since 1900 came close to what Ryne did. Kansas City's George Brett missed out by three stolen bases in 1980. Willie Mays fell short by five hits in 1957.

Stealing bases is hard. Ryne stole 32 in 1984. Then in 1985 he stole 54.

Babe Ruth, Ty Cobb, Ted Williams, Hank Aaron, Reggie Jackson, Pete Rose, and many other great players never came close to what Ryne did. He is a special player.

One team did not realize how good Ryne could be. That was the Philadelphia Phillies.

The Phillies were strong before the 1982 season. They won the World Series in 1980. They would be back in the World Series in 1983. They felt good. They felt all positions except shortstop were good. Their shortstop was an older player named Larry Bowa.

The Phillies liked the Cubs' shortstop, Ivan DeJesus. They wanted to trade with the Cubs for him. They made an agreement. The Cubs would swap DeJesus for Bowa. But, DeJesus was a better player than Bowa. The Phillies seemed to be getting a better deal. They decided to even the trade up. The Phillies also gave the Cubs a 21-year-old infielder. His name was Ryne Sandberg.

Ryne had signed with the Phillies after high school. He had spent four years playing for Philadelphia's minor-league teams. The Phillies must not have thought Ryne would ever be a star. They were wrong.

The Phillies didn't know how good Ryne was when they traded him.

Grown-ups seldom cry. But the people who run the Phillies are grown-ups. They probably cried over losing Ryne.

Think of Ryne today. You think of one of baseball's top hitters. But did you notice that his fielding has also improved?

Ryne was tried at shortstop. He was tried at third base. Then he was put at second base. He became a great player.

A Gold Glove is given to the best fielder at every position in the league. Ryne was given a Gold Glove in his first season at second base.

No other second baseman had ever won a Gold Glove in his first year at the position.

Ryne showed the Cub fans fielding they had not seen in many years. He was the first Cub to win Gold Gloves for two straight years since 1969-70.

Nobody is perfect. But Ryne comes close when he puts on his glove. In 1983 he played 38 games in a row without an error. In 1984 he had 61 straight games without an error. He handled the ball 870 times in 1984. Yet he made only six errors. His record was the best in the National or American League.

People expect so much from Ryne on the field. He just looks like a great athlete. He is 6 feet 2 inches tall. And he is not too heavy at 180

Ryne does not make many fielding errors.

pounds. He fields with grace. He runs like a deer. That is not a surprise. What is a surprise is how he hits the ball.

He almost led the league in total bases in 1984. He missed by one base. (When counting total bases, a single is one; a double, two; a triple, three; and home run, four.) Second basemen are expected to be strong fielders. But most second basemen do not hit well. The last second baseman to lead the National League in total bases did it in 1929.

Ryne was chosen Most Valuable Player of the National League in 1984. A happy Manager Frey said, "No one in the league was more deserving than Ryne."

In 1984 Ryne was named Most Valuable Player of the National League.

A few players thought Keith Hernandes should have been MVP. Keith plays first base for the New York Mets. But Keith agreed with the voters' choice.

"I was hoping to win," Keith said. "But I didn't expect to win. Ryne Sandberg was super. I have no problems finishing second to a player like him."

Ryne was shy before the 1984 season. Reporters would interview him. Ryne would not say more than "yes" or "no." After 1984, he had more to say. Ryne became less shy. He was more confident in himself when he talked.

People expect a lot from Ryne and he delivers.

He also was more confident in his ability to play baseball. He couldn't wait for the 1985 season to start.

"I'm thinking about having a good year." That's what Ryne said before the 1985 season started. "I think I can improve offensively."

He hoped he would improve at batting. Sometimes a pitcher throws a bad pitch. A younger Ryne might not let the bad pitch go by. He would have swung at it.

"I started feeling like a veteran in 1984," he said. "It was just a matter of having a few years under my belt."

Ryne received the Gold Glove for fielding in 1983.

Some players might be a little lazy after having a season like Ryne had in 1984. They might think everything would work out. They might think they had to only half try.

But Ryne knew it wouldn't be that easy. He knew his teammates and the fans. They would expect more from him in 1985. After all, it was the first time he had gone into a season as a star.

He knew pitchers would be harder on him in 1985. They respected him more. They were less likely to let down when he came to bat. They would not want to give him a good pitch to hit.

Yes, Ryne knew how hard it would be.

"It's one thing to have a year like I had in 1984," he said. "But it's another thing to come back and do it two years in a row. For me, it will be just like starting all over again."

Then Ryne went out and proved himself. Players sometimes have one great season. They never play that well again. Not so for Ryne.

He came back in 1985. He batted .305. He ranked with the league leaders. He smashed homers. More homers than he had ever hit. He had 26. He also ranked near the top of the league. He had 186 hits. He had 31 doubles and 54 stolen bases.

Ryne is a triple threat.

He would have driven in more than 83 runs if he had batted fifth or sixth. But he is a good hitter. So he is third in the Cub lineup.

"Since we didn't win the pennant, we wanted to end the season on an up note," Manager Frey said after the season. "Ryne is one of our players who ended the season on an up note."

The entire season was an up note for Ryne. He belted 26 home runs. He stole 54 bases. He again showed that he is a player with rare talent. He was only the third player in baseball history to hit more than 25 home runs and steal more than 50 bases in a season.

Ryne is 6 feet   ches tall and weighs 180 pounds.

Only a "natural" is strong enough to hit more than 25 home runs. Only a "natural" had the speed to steal more than 50 bases. That is Ryne Sandberg.

CHRONOLOGY

1959—Ryne Sandberg is born on September 19 in Spokane, Washington.

1978—Ryne is All-State in football and All-City in both baseball and basketball. He is graduated from Spokane's North Central High School and begins his pro baseball career with the Philadelphia Phillies' farm team in Helena, Montana.

1981—Ryne has an excellent year with the Phillies' farm team in Oklahoma City. He appears headed for the major leagues with the Phillies.

1982—Apparently thinking they already have enough good infielders, in January the Phillies trade Ryne to the Chicago Cubs.

—Ryne starts out poorly with the Cubs, getting only one hit in his first 32 times at bat. When the season ends, he improves enough to be voted the team's best rookie.

1983—After being moved to second base, Ryne wins a Gold Glove. It is the first time a player wins the fielding award in his first season at a position.

1984—Ryne emerges as a great player. He clouts two home runs and drives in seven runs as the Cubs overcome a 7 to 1 St. Louis lead and beat the Cardinals 12 to 11.

—Ryne comes closer than any player ever to have 200 hits, 20 doubles, 20 triples, 20 home runs, and 30 stolen bases in the same season. He falls short by one triple and one home run.

—Ryne leads Chicago to the playoffs for the first time in 39 years.

1985—Just to prove 1984 was no accident, Ryne bats .305, hits 26 home runs and steals 54 bases.

ABOUT THE AUTHOR

Hal Lundgren is a Houston writer who has observed both the inside and the outside of sports. He spent the 1983 season as public relations director of the San Francisco 49ers. During the previous fifteen years, he wrote primarily about pro football, but covered other sports, for the *Houston Chronicle*.

While with the *Chronicle*, Mr. Lundgren was president of the Houston Sportswriters and Sportscasters Association. He served on the Pro Football Hall of Fame Selection Committee and on the board of Big Brothers-Big Sisters of Houston. His other interests include participating in a city basketball league, playing trumpet in a brass ensemble, coaching youth baseball, and following the stock market. He is married and has two sons.

Mr. Lundgren has written five other books in the Sports Stars series: *Earl Campbell: The*

Texas Tornado; Calvin Murphy: The Giant Slayer; Moses Malone: Philadelphia's Peerless Center; Mary Lou Retton: Gold Medal Gymnast; and *Dale Murphy: A Gentleman.*